# MY INTERVIEW SKILLS ARE GOOD

# ...SO WHY DIDN'T I GET A JOB OFFER?

***Easy guide*** for students and recent grads to be ready for an interview that ***gets a job offer!***

STACIE GARLIEB

ISBN: 1449966403
ISBN-13: 9781449966409

# TABLE OF CONTENTS

## *My interview skills are good I think*

## *...so why didn't I get a job offer?©*

---

# INTRODUCTION

Congratulations on having your resume get you to the interview! So now you enter the class of "Interviewing 101". There is homework. This is intended to be a syllabus that will help you work through the process with a targeted amount of research and a set goal at the end – to get the job you want.

The 'we' in the book is referring to a combined collaboration of recruiters, HR managers, and hiring managers who are currently in positions interviewing students and recent grads. 'We' know how interview candidates can answer questions in a complete and interesting way, which makes us want to hire them. We also know what interview candidates could 'crash and burn' – people who didn't know how to be prepared to present themselves well in an interview.

Interviewing is a skill that you develop over time. Practice with your friends, family members, friends of the family, and teachers. The basics are easy, but having skills and flexibility to move between multiple examples throughout your resume make you an exceptional candidate.

• • •

# My interview preparation is complete I think...

Preparing for an interview includes several things, so planning in advance will help you not be stressed out when you find out you have an interview tomorrow. Here's a timeline of some things you can do to be ready:

**To Do Now:**

- Have your resume 'ready to go' on resume paper.
  - Don't worry about getting fancy colored or speckled paper – go with the basic, white resume stock paper. The fabric doesn't matter (linen, cotton, cotton/linen blend) – we aren't going to make sheets out of your resume.

- Get a professional portfolio with a notepad.
  - You will need this for career fairs and live interviews. It's also a good thing to take to networking places like organization (club) meetings with guest speakers who may have internship or job opportunities.

- Buy a suit and shoes that you are comfortable in whether you are standing or sitting.
  - Some interviewers may tell you to dress 'business casual'. That doesn't mean jeans and a button down shirt un-tucked or a

short skirt and sleeveless top. Business casual could be nice pants and a dress shirt without a tie or a knee length skirt with a conservative blouse.

  - Be careful with this though! I have never heard a recruiter or manager mention that someone looked 'too professional' by wearing a suit. Suits tell the interviewer that you are serious about the job and company – it's always better to be over, rather than under, dressed!
  - Choose jewelry that is conservative (no big earrings or necklaces). You will want the interviewer focused on what you are saying, not what you are wearing.

- Figure out answers to basic interview questions – we will talk about this in another section.

**To Do Before a Career Fair:**

- Look at the list of who will be there and plan a strategy.
  - So let's say there are 4 consumer products (think soda) companies who will be there. You don't want to walk over to soda company A and then walk right over to soda company B if their tables are right next to each other. Recruiters watch for things like that, and if you do it, you look like you may be desperate to work for everyone.
    - Walk around to another company in a different area and then come back to soda company B later. Having a plan will make you efficient in how you approach the companies.
  - If the career fair is at school, usually the companies are put in alphabetical order, so that tells you where the tables will be. Career fairs open to the public will have companies 'pay for space' so the bigger ones will be closer to the door, on corners of aisles, and in the biggest areas.

- Figure out when you can go to make the best impact.
    - Basically this means, don't wait until 3:30pm on a Friday if the fair ends at 4pm. Some of the recruiters may be gone by then and you would have missed a chance to meet with them.

- Prepare your resumes and 'one minute sell' – this is explained in detail in the 'Career Fair section'.

**To Do Once You 'Get the Call' to schedule a Phone Interview:**

- Research the company via the internet, business journals, and articles.
  - Know the basics about the company, but please don't memorize the mission statement and annual revenue – the interviewer probably couldn't even repeat those if he had to. Find out some things about the company's latest products/services or technological advancements. What are they doing that is better than the competition? Why do you want to work there – future plans and programs, people in management? (see 'Facebook®/Linked In® section for more info on this)

- Figure out where the best place is for you to be during the phone interview.
  - Ok, so this sounds simple, but you would be surprised how many students and recent grads actually drive down the freeway or walk between classes during a phone interview. Yes, we can tell that when we hear "hey, Jim, did you finish the project?" in the background.
  - Best place to be is always a room that no one else can be in at the same time. If you live with roommates, make sure they don't have access to the area while you are on the phone. You need to be focused and away from distractions.

- Practice your tone of voice with different basic interview questions with a friend or relative.
  - Over the phone we can't see your face so you have to accurately express your emotions with inflection. Obviously having a happy tone when you are explaining your greatest failure would seem a little crazy.

- If you tend to be a quiet or loud talker, the phone will make that more obvious so practice changing your volume accordingly.

**To Do Once You Are Invited for A Live Interview:**

- Plan a route to the location and drive there, even if it's on campus.
  - The day you are interviewing will be the day that the parking lot next to career services is closed, or the road to get to the company's office is shut down with construction, or something else terrible that could make you late for the appointment. Going there the day before will let you make sure you have plenty of time to be EARLY (at least 10 minutes) for the interview.

- Research more about the company – check out the competition, call their customer service department, find out something you didn't know before the phone interview.

- Research who you are interviewing with – look in the 'Facebook®/LinkedIn® section' for more info on this.

- Print out specific resumes
  - The job title and company name should be included in the Objective. Bring at least 3 copies – If we like you, you may get a chance to interview with other people at the same appointment!

- Wear your interview clothes around the house the day before.
  - Remember how comfortable your clothes were in the store? In an interview something will feel too tight, too loose, strange, whatever. You want the interviewer to be listening to what you are saying, not watching you fidget and slouch because of your clothes and shoes.

- Practice answers to interview questions you anticipate getting.
- Prepare your 'Questions to Ask' the interviewer – look in the 'questions at the end of the interview' section for details on this.

• • •

# *My Facebook®/LinkedIn® (social media networking) research is complete I think ...*

Social media networking lets you (and the employer) make contact and find out about each other like never before. Most of you have Facebook®, which can be good and bad. Even if you mark it private, remember that some of your 'friends' or people who have 'tagged' you may not.

Employers are using Facebook® to find out if you have good judgment in general. If your main picture is appropriate (you could show it to your Grandma), then you are ok. Just make sure you don't have anything on your 'wall' that seems extremely unprofessional. Once you start the job search process, you have to be more careful and pay attention to how someone who may want to hire you would perceive the information.

Having said that, as an interview candidate, Facebook® and LinkedIn® are great ways for you to get information about the companies you may want to work for. Here are some general ways you can use both programs:

**Facebook®:**

- Before going to a career fair, look at who is going to be there recruiting for the companies you are planning to visit. Check if the people have a Facebook® profile. You don't care about what their favorite book is - it's just a way for you to recognize their faces before you see them.

- See if the companies you are interested in working for have a Facebook® 'group' page. There may be information on it that won't be on the company website. This also could have events coming up that are open to the public and you could attend and network with people to make contacts!

- Once you get a phone and then live interview, check if the person you will be talking to/meeting with has a page. Now you would want to know a little more about them, but don't memorize anything. Also, don't use things like "I saw that you like animals" in the interview – you will sound like a potential stalker.

**Linked In®:**

- If you are looking for a job and aren't on LinkedIn® – get on it! This program was designed to help business people network. It takes away the dangerous potential of a friend 'writing on your wall' or 'tagging you in a picture' and just lets you put information that is relevant to your school, work, and organizational experiences.

- Make sure you check spelling and grammar for everything you put on your page.

- There are groups for almost any profession that you can search for. Great place to find companies you didn't even think of, especially if you are in special fields (ie: sustainability). Once you find a company, you can go to their company page and get information about who works there and what the company is doing currently in their field.

- In preparation for a career fair, this is another good place to find the company and the recruiters that will be there.

- For phone or live interviews, an interviewer's profile will have information about their work history, career path, and school. This is valuable to help you understand what perspective they may have about the company.

• • •

## *My interview materials are ready to go* I think...

The number one item not to forget for an interview is multiple current copies of your resume. The resume you take to a career fair or live interview needs to have an Objective which includes the company name and title of the job you are interested in. If you don't know what position title to put in, then use a general field of what area you want to work in (sales, management, operations etc.). For more information on how to make your resume tailored to the company, check out ***My resume is perfect* I think*... so why didn't I get the interview?***.

Remember to bring your portfolio and pad of paper – with a pen. This is to carry your resume copies in, and to hold the business cards of the people you meet (so you can follow up with them!). Write some basic questions you want to ask the recruiter or interviewer about the job(s) and/or company on the pad and take notes when they give you the answers.

Please don't bring your backpack or purse to an interview. A professional bag (computer case, briefcase) is completely appropriate. Even though we know you may be a student, a backpack with a suit just doesn't look good. And your XYZ brand clutch bag might be great, but when you are at an interview or career fair it will just sit on the floor, so leave it in the car or a locker. For a career fair, just carry your portfolio with plenty of resume copies.

Leave your cell phone and keys (except your car key) in your car or a locker. You would be surprised how many times we have had a cell phone go off while we are talking to a potential candidate – at career fairs AND interviews. That could be distracting while you are giving the best interview answer of your life!

• • •

# *My career fair interviewing skills make an impact* I think ...

Career fairs can be a great place to make an initial introduction of what skills you can bring to a potential employer. Being prepared will make the process much less painful for you and the recruiters.

- Plan who you are going to see and tailor your resumes to the companies – in your Objective and your bullet points under your experiences.

- Prepare questions in advance to ask the recruiter about the skills they are looking for in candidates in addition to questions about the company.

- Introduce yourself with a firm handshake (don't try to break our hands, though) and good eye contact.

- Give the recruiter a copy of the tailored resume and ask for a business card.
    - Sometimes we will say we don't bring business cards – then you have to get the person's information from career services or the career fair information desk.

- Tell us why you are interested in the company/position, what top skills you can bring to the organization, and where you got the skills. – This is the 'One Minute Sell' of why a recruiter should want to continue to talk to you!

Here's an example:

"Mr. Smith, I am interested in working in the sales team for ABC Company because of your current strategy to increase products in XYZ category for drug store chains. As you can see from my resume, I have previous experience in communicating with customers during my work at Mom's Restaurant where I sold extra menu items like appetizers to more than 100 customers a night. I also have experience in working with teams from my position as the Treasurer in State University Marketing Club, where I collaborated with 8 other board members to coordinate spending of a $5000 budget this past semester. I know that in a sales position with ABC Company being organized would be valuable and I keep organized by using my W Phone and planner."

- Ask what other skills would be important for a qualified candidate in the position. This will tell you where else to go in your school, work, volunteer, or organization experience to tell the recruiter why you would be a good person to interview.

- Find out what the timeline is for the company to schedule interviews – can you schedule one right then?

- Thank the person for their time! We do think that polite students and recent grads would make better employees, so use common courtesy. You will be amazed how far that goes toward considering you for an interview.

- Follow up with the person/people you met from each company within 24 hours. We are probably travelling from school to school or city to city, but we can always check our email. Quick follow up ensures we won't forget you as quickly. Remember to attach the tailored resume when you send the follow up email!

***One note here:***

Don't send any email communication to employers from your SmartPhone. The message may end up getting cut off – then you could look like you don't proofread your work- or the attachment may not go through correctly. Wait and send any documents to companies from a computer to make sure it goes through completely.

• • •

## *My phone interviewing skills will get me a live interview* I think...

So, why do interviewers do phone interviews first in some cases? Outside of school and career services, phone interviews let us get to talk with you for a little amount of time to see if you have good communication skills, if you know what we are looking for in a candidate, and if you have the skills to be successful in the job. Phone interviews give a quick view of whether you are qualified enough to make it to the face-to-face interview.

Most phone interviews are short so you need to make a big impact in a little amount of time. Here are your objectives for the phone interview as a candidate:

- Create an interest for the interviewer to keep talking to you more about your background and skills.
- Get more information on what skills the organization is looking for.
- Describe your examples of having those skills.
- Discover the timeline for filling the position and what the next steps in the process will be.

  and most importantly –

- Secure a face-to-face interview appointment with them or another person in the organization.

Very few people get hired just over the phone, so if you don't ask for a face-to-face interview while you have them on the phone, you may lose your chance at getting the job!

The first point sounds easy, but is the one that takes the most planning and preparation. If you have done your homework (refer to the 'Interview Preparation section') ahead of time on what skills the company is looking for, you can make a quick impact with just a few brief sentences.

What is the most common question interviewers ask first? It's pretty much the same for phone and face-to-face interviews, and each interviewer will ask it differently:

"Why are you interested in this position?"
"What about this position is interesting to you?"
"Why do you want to work for ABC Company?"
or the most direct way –
"Why are you here today?"

Basically we want you to explain 'what's in it for ME', as the interviewer, to keep talking to you and hear what you bring to the organization from skills and experience. As a student or recent grad, you may not have a lot of practical experience in the exact field you are interviewing for, so you need to focus on skills that you have gotten in school, volunteer, organization (club), or work experiences.

Take the list in the back (***SUCCESSFUL IMPRESSIONS*** Phone Interview Questions ©) and write down your answers in this format:

**Situation**

- What happened to start the example you are giving?

"In my CSI 201 class we had a group project with five people that included a powerpoint presentation to the class and paper that we turned in at the end of the semester which counted for 40% of my grade."

**Task**

- What specifically did you do to make the example happen?

"I set a timeline with the group for when we would have meetings to update each other on the separate research we were doing. My section of the paper was on how planets align during Fall months, so I used the internet, articles in newspapers, and personal stories from astronomers to accumulate information prior to each meeting."

**Action**

- During the example, what steps did you take to make sure things were improved, moved forward, completed on time, etc?

"At each meeting, I reported on my section's research and asked for feedback from group members. I also checked that each person was meeting the timeline and then showed their work. I offered to create the powerpoint and asked each person to get me their ideas for slides two months in advance of the deadline so we could collaborate and make changes if needed. I began working on the powerpoint and found video and audio to complement our topic and inserted that in also."

**Result**

- What specific goals and/or objectives were achieved?

"Our group met our timeline for each of the parts of the project. I put the initial powerpoint together and then we reviewed it as a group and made a few updates. We practiced our presentation two weeks before it was scheduled. All of our preparation and work paid off because we received an A on the project and I got an A in the class."

The **STAR** format makes recruiters VERY happy to hear for two key reasons. First, by telling us a 'story' with a 'beginning – the situation', 'middle – tasks and actions', and 'ending – results', we can take really specific notes on what skills you have and how you have used them. Second, several companies (most of the Fortune 500 at least) have adapted the **STAR** format (behavioral-based interviewing) as what interviewers will ask for in answers. This format takes away some of the subjective part in interviewing. If your answers always follow this format, the interviewer can easily determine what skills you have and how they may be valuable to their organization.

***Two 'watch-outs' of Phone Interviews:***

1) Be conscious of 'ums' and long pauses – these are very obvious over the phone. If you are someone who says 'like' a lot – that could be another word to try and limit.
    - One way to avoid these is to repeat the question back to the interviewer to give yourself time to think of a good example.

2) Be specific in your answers – don't wander into theoretical situations such as
   "If I had a job with ABC Company, I would....". Interviewers want to know what you have done in the past that is the most similar to what behavior or skill we are looking for.

The next step is to find out what the company's timeline is for filling the position. Easiest way to find this out is to just ask:

"What is your timeline for interviewing candidates for this position and hiring?"

You need to know this so you can keep track of when to follow up and find out where you are in the process.

Finally, ask for a face-to-face interview. This is not being too forward or pushy. If you don't ask us for the next step, we don't feel like we have to necessarily give it to you! Once you have had a chance to answer the questions in the STAR format completely, you earn the right to ask to move forward in the process.

• • •

## *My face-to-face interview answers are ready and specific to the position*

....

---

In the last section, we talked about how to answer questions using the **STAR** format in phone interviews. Use the same format for face-to-face interviews! Here's the big difference – the interviewer is sitting right there so you have to show your confidence in the answers. The process is a little different too, more similar to the career fair format but longer:

- Introduce yourself, hand the interviewer a current copy of your tailored resume, and ask for a business card.

- Sit down and don't get too comfortable – don't slouch or fidget or make it obvious you are nervous by putting your hands on top of the table or desk.

- Keep good eye contact.
  - Please don't stare at the interviewer, it is strange. Also bad to 'check in' with your eyes and then dart them around the room nervously. Just relax and look away occasionally like you would in a normal conversation.

- Use appropriate tone and volume for the location – don't shout if you are in an office like you may need to if you are at XYZ Coffee Store.

At this point, you may have met the interviewer before at a career fair or over the phone or at a club meeting. If that is the case, you should still not call them by their first name until they tell you to. It is always better to call someone Mr. or Ms. Smith.

So if you have spoken to this person before and given them some information about your skills and examples using the STAR format, what happens when they ask you the same question, or a question in the same category that you want to give an example you already used? Two options – one is to mention that you talked about the example before but then give some new details about how that example shows your skills, the other option is to have another example ready!

In the back of the book is a list for you to write your answers to common categories of interview questions. Each list has a heading to show you what the overall skill the interviewer is looking for with those particular questions. Take the list (***SUCCESSFUL IMPRESSIONS*** Categorized Interview Questions©) and pick a couple of questions from each category and write your answers in STAR format. Use school, work, volunteer, organization (club), and other experiences that make you 'stand out' from other candidates. The more answers you can use in different areas of your life, the better the interviewer can understand how those skills could be used in their company!

***Face-to-Face Interview 'Not To Do's:***

- Don't become relaxed in your speech and use slang. 'Chill' does not explain anything relevant to your skills for a potential employer.

- Be careful not to use vague 'Miss America' examples that talk about 'you' or 'the people'.
    - If your answers could end with 'solve world hunger' or 'create world peace', then they are not specific enough and probably didn't use the STAR format.
    - 'I', 'me', and 'we' are the only pronouns allowed in an answer for an interview
        - If an answer uses 'you' then the content just shifted into talking about the interviewer which is odd and inappropriate.

• • •

## *My questions at the end of the interview are smart and strategic I think ....*

At the end of EVERY interview, the last question from the interviewer is:

"What questions do you have about (the position, the company etc.)?"

The wrong answer to this question is – "I don't really have any questions."

There is no possible way that you know everything about the job, the company, the expectations for the position within the organization, the goals of the company in short and long term etc. Candidates who answer that they don't have any questions just look unprepared for the interview, whether it's over the phone or in person.

So, what are good questions to ask? Depends on the company, what the position is, what stage you are at in the interview process, and who you are interviewing with. No ONE question is good or bad to ask every interviewer.

***One note:***

Salary and benefits questions are not appropriate to ask until you have been given a job offer. In most cases, there is some way to find out that information 'behind the scenes' through career services or online on the company's internal website. Some companies will inform candidates about those details in information sessions too, so make sure if there is an opportunity to attend one of those you do!

Here are some general things to consider as you choose questions to ask an interviewer:

- What questions do you want to know in order to determine whether you want to work at the company?
  - Think about asking about technology used, expansion plans, growth in certain areas

- Have you talked with this interviewer before – what questions did you ask them then?
  - Please don't ask us the same question over again – we do notice that and it sounds bad.

- What role does the interviewer play in the organization?
  - Someone who is your potential boss would be a good person to ask about expectations for the next year in the job.

- Can you find out more general information about the company and the management from this person?
  - Questions about company culture and overall management style are good ones.

- Did you ask the same question to someone else in the organization?
  - It's ok to ask three different people (at different interviews or in a group interview setting) the same question – but

you need to acknowledge that you are asking the same question:

> "I asked Mr. Smith about his career path in XYZ Company, could you tell me what your experience in the company has been that led you to your current role?"

Just make certain your questions have a purpose and that you can use the information to expand your knowledge of the organization as well as what the position needs to do for the company!

• • •

## *My 'final question' answers where I stand in the interview process* I think....

After you ask a couple – three or four are ok too as long as you are considerate of the interviewer's time – of questions to get more information on specifics about the company or position, the last question needs to be your 'closing question'. A closing question lets you ask:

- To move to the next step in the interview process
  - You need to find out what this is first, so the question before needs to ask what the next step is!
- What additional training or skills you need to get the job
  - This will tell you what you didn't explain well enough in your interview answers or what you need to 'prove' to the interviewer that would make you a good person to hire.
- Is there more information in a certain area that you need to provide
  - If you didn't give STAR answers, watch out – interviewers can be brutal on this one....
- Did you answer the questions completely enough to show your skills fit the job, and will you be considered a top candidate to be hired for the job

The more shy candidates are going to be scared to use the last one. Here's the good news, you only pick ONE final question, not more than one. Go with a phrasing that will work for your personal style. The point is to ask for action on the part of the interviewer and to find out where you stand in the process. It's amazing how many students and recent grads have walked out of interviews and said 'I think they liked me'. Not good enough if you want to be a competitive candidate who gets the job you want.

So, what's the worst thing that could happen – the interviewer could tell you that your answers weren't specific enough, your skills don't match the job, you aren't 'what we are looking for'. Then you can find out what you did wrong and do better next time! Interviewing isn't brain science – it takes practice and learning how to get better every time in representing yourself accurately with what skills you have. You can't date every person at school, and you aren't a fit for every company – that is ok. The 'closing question' helps you be a better interview candidate for the next company.

• • •

## *My follow up skills position me for a job offer*  ....

As interviewers, we appreciate the candidates who take time to acknowledge OUR time in the interview process. Even though sending an email right after an interview seems like a 'no brainer', it's amazing how many students and recent grads don't do it. Please follow up, and when you do, here are some guidelines:

- Write a follow up email within 24 hours of meeting a potential employer
    - It doesn't matter if you met them at a club meeting, career fair, networking event, phone interview, or face-to-face interview – follow up EVERY time with EVERY person.

- If possible, handwrite a note after in person interviews and send or fax it within 24 hours.
    - If the company is in town then you can also hand deliver it. Handwritten notes add a special personalization to the interview process and can show extra initiative on the part of the candidate.

- Depending on the timeline you found out during your questioning the interviewer or recruiter, make a follow up phone call a week after the written or email note.

- To do this effectively, it's important to take good notes on when the company is going to 'get back to qualified candidates'. You don't want to seem like a pain and call them before the timing they told you.

Job candidates who do consistent follow up have a greater chance of being hired if their skills are a match. Excessive follow up can be obnoxious so be careful to respect the information the interviewer gave you about the company's timeline. Also be aware that the timeline could change, so show understanding about that as well. Once you have talked to the person after the initial written communication, switch back and forth between written and verbal follow up to see what is easiest for the person to get back to you on – every recruiter and interviewer is different.

• • •

# *My interview skills are good* I think *...so why didn't I get a job offer?©*

---

Here's a final checklist to help you make sure you are ready for an interview that gets you an offer:

- ✓ Your resume has the title and company name in the Objective tailored for each company
  - o Tells them that you know what and who you are applying for and to

- ✓ Suit, portfolio with pad, resume paper all purchased and ready to go
- ✓ Before the career fair you have researched and planned who to visit
  - o Use social media and the internet for the company and recruiter information

- ✓ Before the phone interview–practice your questions, tone, and prepare questions to ask
  - o Plan your research and location

- ✓ Before the face-to-face interview–practice your questions, update your questions to ask
  - o Wear your interview clothes, drive to the location, get tailored resume copies ready

- ✓ Practice asking your 'closing question' to friends, family, etc
  - o If you already have asked it, you will be less nervous to ask an interviewer over the phone or in person

- ✓ After EVERY meeting with a potential employer send a follow up communication
  - o Separate yourself from the competition by being courteous

- ✓ Follow up consistently and be patient if the timeline for hiring changes

Now you are ready to start your preparation! Use the lists and checklists to make the interview process less intimidating and more of an opportunity for you to show employers what skills you can offer to their Company.
Be confident in the interview process–no one (not even your parents) knows you and what skills you have more than you do. Prepare, plan, practice, and interviewers will appreciate the talent you have and will be ready to hire you!

# *SUCCESSFUL IMPRESSIONS*

## *PHONE INTERVIEW QUESTIONS ©*

1. **What about working for ABC Company interests you?**

2. **How do you believe your education has helped you to be prepared for this position?**

3. **Tell me about some of the jobs you've held in the past and how they have helped to prepare you for this position.**

4. **How did you decide on your major?**

5. **What projects have you worked on in the past that are similar to this position?**

6. **How have you organized your time in school and work?**

7. **What computer skills do you have and where have you used them?**

8. **Tell me about a time that you had to juggle several activities at once.**

9. **How do you prioritize your activities?**

10. **Tell me about a time that you had to help a group to meet a common goal.**

11. **What are you looking for in a position?**

12. **What aspects of your past jobs have you liked the most? The least?**

13. **Tell me about a recent accomplishment that you have had in the past year.**

14. **What interests or hobbies do you have outside of school and work?**

15. **What is the most difficult decision you have had to make and why?**

• • •

# *SUCCESSFUL IMPRESSIONS*

## CATEGORIZED INTERVIEW QUESTIONS ©

### MOTIVATION

Tell me about a time you did something that needed to be done, but it was not your responsibility.

Give me an example of a time you had to produce results without being given direction or guidelines.

What motivates you and why?

Tell me about a significant project or task where you really went the "extra mile" to achieve it.

What types of rewards will motivate you to work extra hard at your job?

Tell me about a couple of goals you set for yourself (aside from graduation), why they were important to you, and what you did to achieve them.

Tell me about a time when, despite your hard work, you failed to achieve the results you expected.

**How to you motivate yourself to accomplish significant yet distasteful tasks?**

**Tell me about a time that you put more time and effort into a project than was necessary; what caused you to work harder than you needed to?**

**What was the most unpleasant task you were assigned in work or school; how long did you wait to begin working on it and how long did it take for you to finish the assignment?**

**Tell me about the last time you found yourself with nothing to do; how did you go about filling your time?**

**Describe the last project you worked on that required large amounts of overtime.**

**Describe the most boring project you have ever worked on; how did it turn out?**

**Describe a time you had to learn and apply a new procedure or skill.**

• • •

## *SUCCESSFUL IMPRESSIONS*
## CATEGORIZED INTERVIEW QUESTIONS ©

### COMMUNICATION SKILLS

Tell me about the most complicated formal presentation you have had to make at school or on the job; who was there, what did you do to prepare, how did you organize the presentation, what was the most trying moment of the presentation for you, and what was the outcome?

What do you see as your strengths and weaknesses when it comes to conveying ideas orally?

Tell me about a time that you used effective communication to resolve a problem with a customer or co-worker.

What was the most enjoyable writing assignment you had and why?

How do you rate your ability to express your ideas and opinions to others?

• • •

# *SUCCESSFUL IMPRESSIONS*
# CATEGORIZED INTERVIEW QUESTIONS ©

## JUDGMENT and DECISION MAKING

**Describe the last situation where you had to "think on your feet".**

**How do you typically approach problems?**

**What do you see as your strongest and weakest points as a decision maker? Why?**

**Tell me about a time you had to make a quick decision when you did not have all the information you wanted.**

**Give me an example of a time you made the wrong decision.**

**How do you determine when you have gathered and analyzed sufficient data to make a decision?**

**Tell me about the most complex decision you have made where there were many details and alternatives to consider; what were your alternatives, what were the pros and cons of each alternative, how did you decide on a final solution?**

**Tell me about the last time you made a decision that backfired; what caused you to choose that course of action, what options**

**did you consider, what feedback did you get, what did you learn from the experience?**

**How do you combine your intuition and "gut feelings" with factual evidence when making a decision?**

• • •

## *SUCCESSFUL IMPRESSIONS*
## CATEGORIZED INTERVIEW QUESTIONS ©

### SELF-CONFIDENCE

**What are your strengths and why?**

**What are your weaknesses and why?**

**Tell me about the last time you took and unpopular stand on an issue at work or school.**

**Describe a situation when you made a sacrifice because you felt the long-term result would make it worthwhile.**

**Describe the last time you were criticized by your superior; how did you handle it?**

**Describe a situation that demonstrates your confidence in your abilities at your job. Has anyone ever been critical of your performance in this area?**

• • •

*SUCCESSFUL IMPRESSIONS*

## CATEGORIZED INTERVIEW QUESTIONS ©

### RELIABILITY

**Tell me about the last time you let someone important down.**

**What do you do when you have an important decision to make?**

**Tell me about the last time you were commended for getting something done.**

**What commitments do you have to meet in your job; what are you most proud of in relation to meeting your commitments?**

**What has been the hardest time you have had coming to work; why was it hard and what did you do?**

**When was the last time you were really counted on?**

**What are your expectations about the job and the company?**

• • •

# *SUCCESSFUL IMPRESSIONS*
# CATEGORIZED INTERVIEW QUESTIONS ©

## FLEXIBILITY and ADAPTABILITY

**What school/work experiences have you had which required you to work at a fast pace under stress?**

**Describe the most radical change in your work environment that you have gone through.**

**Describe the last situation in which you were confronted with a sudden and unexpected change in plans.**

**How do you handle stress?**

**How much supervision/help do you typically seek when faced with a difficult problem?**

**Describe the last time you established a plan and were forced to change it.**

**What boss did you find easiest to work for and why?**

**Tell me about the most difficult transition you have had to make.**

**Tell me about the last time you really got mad about something.**

**Tell me about an instance when you have had to confront someone; what position were you and the other person in?**

**Describe a situation where you disagreed with someone while at work; how was the disagreement solved?**

**Tell me about a time you had to ask for assistance when completing a project.**

**Describe a time when you had to change the way you accomplish a task in order to interact more effectively with someone very different from you; what did you do to adapt?**

• • •

# *SUCCESSFUL IMPRESSIONS*
# CATEGORIZED INTERVIEW QUESTIONS ©

## CUSTOMER SERVICE/INTERPERSONAL SKILLS

**Tell me about three characteristics you feel are important for effective customer service.**

**What are your strengths in dealing with people?**

**What are your weaknesses in dealing with people?**

**Describe the toughest customer or other person you have had to deal with; what did the person say or do, what did you say or do, what was the result?**

**Tell me about a time you had trouble selling a product or an idea; what obstacles did you run into?**

**When was the last time you had to deal with an angry customer on your present job?**

**Describe the last time you handled a complaint on the part of a customer or a situation where there was potential for losing a customer.**

• • •

## TIME MANAGEMENT

**In managing work and school, how do you determine your priorities?**

**Tell me about a time you were unable to meet a deadline.**

**How do you organize your work and schedule your time?**

**When do you decide what to do each day?**

**How do you plan the amount of time you will spend on each task when you do them?**

**What has been the biggest challenge in making effective use of your time?**

**Give me an example of using your time effectively was a problem.**

**Tell me about the most significant time where you were "bogged down" with a lot of tasks to accomplish in a short amount of time.**

• • •

# *SUCCESSFUL IMPRESSIONS*
# CATEGORIZED INTERVIEW QUESTIONS ©

## ORGANIZATION

**Describe the last mistake you made involving details because you were rushed to meet a deadline; what was the error, what effect did the mistake have, what feedback did you receive?**

**What was the toughest deadline you have had to meet recently, what little things did you sacrifice to meet it, what mistakes or omissions did others find?**

**Tell me about the last time you were commended for efficiently handling a number of small details.**

**How do you handle large amounts of paperwork without becoming bogged down in irrelevant detail?**

**Describe an assignment which required you to take care of the greatest number of details; how did you proceed and what steps did you take to ensure that these details were taken care of?**

**Describe the steps you typically take to meet deadlines.**

**Tell me about the job which presented the biggest challenge in terms of organizing information and scheduling your time.**

• • •

## *SUCCESSFUL IMPRESSIONS*
## CATEGORIZED INTERVIEW QUESTIONS ©

### LEADERSHIP

**What experience do you have leading people? What types of roles were they in?**

**What were your biggest challenges in a leadership role?**

**Tell me about a time that you had to change your interpersonal style to accommodate the needs of those on your team project?**

**What are your strengths as a leader and why?**

**What are your weaknesses as a leader and why?**

**Tell me about a situation when you had an individual on your team who was not participating; what did you do and what were the results?**

**What is your natural leadership style; time keeper, organizer, idea person, coordinator, devil's advocate?**

• • •

## Extra Resources:

**Career Services/Career Center Departments**

- Depending on the college or university, you may have access to classes on interviewing or 'mock interview' sessions.

**www.bestresumebuilder.com**

- If you want to use a program which will walk you through, step by step, in less than a half hour, check out this resource. Created specifically for collegiates and recent grads, it's specific and easy to use. This may help you focus your interview answers to the 'bullet points' on your resume.

**Other Interviewing Skills Books**

- For specific ideas on answering questions and preparation in specific fields, there are resources on professional affiliation and organization websites.

• • •

# Index



• • •

***Other Books in the I think Career Skills Series:***

***Available Online and In Stores February 2010!***

Acknowledgements

For the students who have listened and taken the information forward over the past 20 years to create amazing career opportunities – thank you for teaching me how to make the 'basics' create successful experiences for anyone. To the KDs – thanks for the sisterly support through online and college campus experiences. To the 'managers' who listened in the past, thank you for taking the interviewing and hiring skills forward to help others.

To the Board of CSS – thank you for the patience to make our vision move forward through these projects.
To Mark – thank you for being patient and understanding while the creative mind interacts with the corporate.
To Tyler for double-checking my work, always being my favorite student, and teaching me more than anyone else ever could have.

• • •

## *About the Author*

Stacie Garlieb is the author of 'My resume is perfect I think ... so why didn't I get the interview?'©. As the President of Successful Impressions, LLC., she assists collegiates and recent graduates with career search processes and skills. She has been featured several times on NBC television and KFYI radio during morning and evening news with interview tips. In partnership with University of Phoenix, Stacie is the creator and presenter for the 'Career Workshop Series' on resume building, interview preparation, interview skills, social media networking, and 're-careering' and transition in the workforce.

Stacie has been a seminar speaker for 'Build Your Career Event' (Career Builder/University of Phoenix) and the Arizona Women's Expo. Her career search tips and interview skills advice have been published in national sorority and university alumni publications. Through group presentations and one-on-one coaching on all career search related topics, she has worked with public and private college students nationally since 1991. In collaboration with businesses in various fields, she actively develops internship programs and recruits at public and private universities as well as career fairs.

Stacie was invited by California State Sacramento and University of the Pacific to act as a Career Consultant to the career services departments. She developed the Career Fair Training Program for University of the Pacific, and assisted in writing the "Career Services Interview Skills" guide. Over more than twenty years, she has worked for Fortune 500 organizations in sales, marketing, and management positions with recruiting responsibility after earning her Bachelor of Science from Arizona State University.

*If you would like to know more about Stacie Garlieb's company or her seminars please visit her website at www.successfulimpressions.net*

LaVergne, TN USA
31 January 2011
214670LV00007B/178/P